The Birth of a Mother

AF624502

Candice Graham

BookLeaf Publishing

The Birth of a Mother © 2023 Candice Graham

All rights reserved.

No part of this publication may be reproduced, stored in a retrieval system, or transmitted, in any form or by any means, electronic, mechanical, photocopying, recording or otherwise, without the prior written permission of the presenters.

Candice Graham asserts the moral right to be identified as author of this work.

Presentation by *BookLeaf Publishing*

Web: www.bookleafpub.com

E-mail: info@bookleafpub.com

ISBN: 9789357212489

First edition 2023

DEDICATION

For Annalee and William because without you I would have never experienced the wild journey that is motherhood.

A Positive?

Panic, fear, excitement,
Pain, frustration, or joy
Which is right ?
What is the correct response
to a positive line ?

How can one comprehend
all the change that is ahead?
But yet in an instant it all flashes before me
And I am forced to respond.

My brain is foggy, it is scared.
It sees no way to manage,
No way to balance.
Only stress and troubles ahead.

But my heart,
My heart is strangely gleeful.
Full to the brim with emotion
Bursting in ways I never thought possible.

So though I am unsure,
Though I am confused,
I must trust my heart and the one who formed it
That this is all good news.

My World

You have always been my world
From the day we met.
My heart was made to be with yours
So the wedding date was set.

Because of this I feared the change,
The growth from two to three.
How would we survive
When it is more than you and me?

But then came her
And I knew once more
That she was made for me.
So much love bubbled out
From deep inside my core.

In a moment my world it grew
And there was room for two.
Two perfect souls made just for me,
Annalee and you.

What’s in a name?

There is one thing no one tells you about
parenthood.

It isn’t the late nights,
Or the smell of vomit.
It isn’t the cost of nappies,
Or the mess of dinner time.

It’s the difficulty of choosing a name.

How does one pick the right name
for a person they have just met?
What name could possibly be good enough
To represent the amazing being that is in your
arms.

What name has no negative connotations
But is still strong enough to speak on behalf of
your child?

Why does no one discuss the high stakes that
come with choosing a child’s name?

Calm

The noise is constant.

The thoughts
The lists
The buzz

The fear
The worry
The pain

Until you hold me

Then it's not

It's calm
and safe
and quiet.

Chaos

I used to say I loved chaos
That chaos was my friend.
The hustle and the bustle
I prayed it'd never end.

But then I had a toddler
Who planned chaos in her sleep.
And now the thought of it
Really makes me weep.

I wish I just had one small day
Where things all went to plan.
Where we ate and napped in quiet
And didn’t play with sand.

Space

I had a dream last night.

I dreamt of the most wonderful thing,
Something I could only ever dream of.

It caught my eye instantly
drawing me into its wonder.
Something so rare, so affluent.
Yet in my dream I had more than I could fathom.

As I sit feeding I cannot help but imagine it.
Over the toddler screaming and the baby crying
I hear it calling out to me.
Oh how I long to obtain what I dreamt of last
night.
How I wish to fill my house with it.
Even just a drop would suffice.
Oh how I wish I had a little space
like I dreamt of last night.

Mummy Brain

You hear it said over and over again
"Don't worry dear it's just mum brain".
Since having kids there is a blur
It's continual presence makes me feel insaine.

But I have a theory.
It is not because of brain shrinkage
Or sleep deprevation
Or hormone imbalances.

I believe this blur is far far more.
See our brains are only built for one
But a mother's has to hold it all
Her children have not made her dumb

She is smarter now than ever before
She can balance the needs of all her children
She knows their wants, their aches, their pains
She keeps them all in her brain with no problem.

Sleep

Something gone for years
How my heart longs for it now
One day I will sleep.

Little Love

Little teeth and a little toes
Little eyes and a little nose
Little curls and little ears
Little fingers and a little mouth

But my love for you is far from little
Just like your sweet cheek dimple

Dear second child

I am sorry that I put you down
and have to let you cry.

I am sorry that your toys aren't new
and your nappy's still not dry.

You see your mum is pretty thin strung
and your sister is a handful.

It doesn't mean I love you less
Or think you're harder to handle.

Two under two is more than I knew
But there is no doubt I love you too.

Babies Bounce

At two days old my tired hands dropped you,
I cried for hours but they whispered to me,
“It's ok don't you know that babies bounce”

When he first held you fear filled his eyes
He did not want to hurt you. I simply said,
“He‘ll be alright babies always bounce”

When your sister runs at you with top speeds
And jumps into your chair. I sigh with great
relief,
“Thankyou Jesus for making babies bounce”.

More than cry

I wish my kids did more than cry
Like talk or dance or sing
Oh wait I've got that wrong way round
I think I've lost my mind

My kids wish I did more than cry
Like talk or dance or sing
But sorry guys, I'm all used up
I can't do anything

I’ve lost myself

I've lost my socks, I've lost my bag
My head hurts and my boobs sag
I can't remember my own birth date
And now my hearings second rate

I've swollen ankles and tummy troubles
And my thoughts are lost among the rubble
They tell me I'll get used to this, the mom's who have it right
But right now I'd like to have a nap and there's no nap in sight

I think it's worth it, I really do
When I come around and look at you
But I'm sore and tired and can't think straight
Will you go to sleep before it's late?

More than this

I feel like I was once more than this
More than nappies and dirty bottles
More than the one who stays at home
I feel like I was more capable on my own

And yet I feel like I need to do more than this
More cleaning than I currently do
More helping in and around the home
I feel like I am truly failing in this zone

I don't know how to be more than this
More than who I am
I am trying my hardest everyday
To be the best mum I can.

Drama

Today my toddler cried for hours
All I did was peel a banana
She did not want it open you see
I clearly am the source of drama

Life lost

Life lost yet life gained
Motherhood is a strange being
I miss who was before

The joy

I know I complain a lot
But please take it with a grain of salt
Beneath the screams and cries of stress
I really do think they're the best.

Nothing can explain it truly
Just how much they mean to me
The joy bursting in my heart
Was made by them like a work of art.

Go and Take a Nap

If this book you've read in full
You're putting something off.
Although I'm glad you read it all
It's really not top notch.

Don't worry I won't dob you in
I won't even tell my dog
Cause if the truth is being told
I'm with you in that bog.

So while we're both ignoring chores
Just go and take a nap
And just incase you haven't heard
The patriarchy's cap.

www.ingramcontent.com/pod-product-compliance
Lightning Source LLC
Chambersburg PA
CBHW051723130826
49812CB00034B/1316
9789357212489